In July 1901 five railway companies raced one another to bring daytime Anglo-Scottish expresses to their destination, utilising three different routes. It was a week which saw timetables being torn up, locomotives being run as fast they could go, questions asked in the House of Commons about rail safety, and dastardly goings-on at a certain rail junction where two expresses were racing to be first . . .

This is a true story, told in book form for the first time.

An official shot of Midland Railway simple 4-4-0 No. 2607, one of Johnson's "Belpaire" locomotives built at the dawn of the Twentieth Century and largely eclipsed by the same designer's Compounds. Nevertheless, these locomotives were no slouches in their brief sojourn on the Settle-Carlisle line. Note the large-capacity eight-wheel tender — any unscheduled stop for water, as happened one day during the 1901 Race — was certain to result in defeat. (W. E. Boyd collection)

THE RAILWAY RACE TO SCOTLAND

1901

By A.J. Mullay

MOORFOOT PUBLISHING
EDINBURGH

ISBN 0 906606 13 6

Cover design by Tony Steers.

This Book is dedicated to
John M. Saunders,
(1946-1985)
Much-missed Colleague and Friend.

Published in 1987 by Moorfoot Publishing,
PO Box 506,
SW Postal District,
Edinburgh 10.

Printed by Waddington & Sons (Printers) Ltd.,
Fielden Square,
Todmorden,
Lancashire.

CONTENTS

FOREWORD

As she pounded through the Moorfoot hills, the destination of Edinburgh coming ever nearer, it was obvious that No 738 was making up lost time. Despite leaving Carlisle nine minutes late, the North British 4-4-0 and her determined crew were well on the way to achieving a punctual arrival in the Scottish capital.

But that might not be enough. The North Eastern were due to bring the *Flying Scotsman* into Edinburgh at about the same time as 738 was scheduled to arrive with her train, the 09.30 from St Pancras. Who would be first to reach the "finishing line" at Portobello East Junction that windy Monday in July 1901? Not the North Eastern if 738 could help it!

Topping Falahill summit in 105 minutes from Carlisle, the North British train reeled off the remaining fourteen miles to the junction at a mile a minute – about the highest speed possible on the Waverley Route, a main-line notorious for its curves and summits. Portobello East, the junction of the two lines from London, inched closer as the driver strained to see the signals at Niddrie, the last signalbox before Portobello. All signals were "off" for the vital junction!

With excitement mounting among the train's passengers, 738 swept through the East junction with no sign of a train from the North Eastern direction. A near-punctual arrival seemed almost certain, despite the late start from Carlisle. Was the North British first into its spiritual home, Edinburgh?

There were only three and a half miles to go.

Seven of the first eight days of July 1901 witnessed some of the most exciting "racing" in British railway history, yet little of it has been recorded, and most historians seem to have ignored it. Such authors as O.S. Nock and Cecil J. Allen have dismissed the events of 1901 as being unimportant and unworthy of discussion. The former denies that the Portobello signalman was ever required to offer the road to one racing express while holding back another which had reached him at the same time, (see *The Railway Race to the North*), although there is in fact evidence that something of this kind actually happened. The latter is openly contemptuous of the North British performance in 1901, (see *The North Eastern Railway*), despite every indication that the Scottish company's performance was impaired by the inability of its partner, the Midland, to operate fast long-distance expresses efficiently.

In fact, the Midland's notorious record for performing unpunctually on its Anglo-Scottish services, was what prompted the North Eastern to re-time the northbound *Flying Scotsman* in the first place, thus setting off the events of July 1901. But there were other factors involved and it is perhaps worthwhile to investigate these before proceeding to the story of the 1901 Railway Race to Edinburgh.

Why should the North Eastern and the North British, both members of the East Coast consortium, along with the Great Northern, be racing against each other? Why did the West Coast companies make a meteoric appearance in the race later that week? Why was there a race at all?

HISTORICAL BACKGROUND

There had been two previous outbursts of racing between London and Scotland – in 1888 to Edinburgh, and in 1895 to Aberdeen. In the former year London-Edinburgh traffic was contested between the East Coast companies (Great Northern and North Eastern) on one side and the West Coast (London and North Western and Caledonian) on the other.

Previously unprecedented travelling times between the capital cities of 7 hours 27 minutes (East) and 7 hrs 38 mins (West) were achieved, inclusive of stops for passengers' meals and for locomotive purposes. In theory, the East Coast partners won the race, although the indeterminate, unpredictable, nature of meal-stops played havoc with time saved by hard running. Some of the most determined performances came from the West Coast, with its slightly longer route, and its three summits of Shap, Beattock, and Cobbinshaw.

So impressive was locomotive working on both routes to Scotland that summer that it would be invidious to commend individual perform-ances and ignore others. Yet the Caledonian Railway, the only active Scottish participant, can only be admired for its cavalier contribution to the West Coast effort. In the form of single-wheeler No 123, now happily preserved in Glasgow's Museum of Transport, the round-100 mile Carlisle-Edinburgh (Princes Street) dash, with its two gruelling summits, was being run day after day in splendid style. 123 averaged 107 minutes for this distance over no fewer than twenty-three journeys, with a slowest time of 110 minutes and a peak performance of 102½ minutes, admittedly with a lightweight load. With larger four-driving-wheel locomotives already the staple for express passenger trains, 123's panache was almost the last salute to a past era of railways.

3

Seven years later, racing overnight to Aberdeen, the East Coast allies were joined by their hitherto sleeping partner, the North British, over whose metals the NER exercised running powers from Berwick-upon-Tweed to Edinburgh, but which then entered the rivalry for the first time, competing with the Caledonian on the final stretch to Aberdeen. Unlike 1888, when the racing trains terminated in different stations a mile apart at each end of Edinburgh's Princes Street, the 1895 race was characterised by a single "winning post", at Kinnaber Junction, a signal-box thirty-eight miles south of the Granite City.

Portobello East Junction, three and a half miles east of Edinburgh Waverley, was to be the "Kinnaber Junction" of 1901 and enjoyed a similarly important strategic position in relation to Edinburgh. Its 45-lever box on the down (south) side controlled this important joining of two routes from London, as well as the turn-out from the Portobello yards. Although the location was still very sylvan, this only served to disguise the congestion experienced by rail traffic at this point. Within fifteen years, the NBR had built a complex of lines – the Lothian Lines – to bypass the area and relieve the pressure on Portobello East, where a large overhead signal-box was erected in 1909.

Yet there was one important difference between Kinnaber and the Edinburgh junction. The East Coast and Waverley main-lines joining at Portobello were *both* North British! Why then was the local company having to compete with another, but on its own metals? The answer to that is crucial to an understanding of the 1901 incidents.

Since 1862 the North Eastern had enjoyed the right of running express trains straight into Waverley station, even although that company's own metals stretched only as far as the north end of the Royal Border Bridge at Berwick-upon-Tweed. This privilege was actively taken up in 1869, while in exchange the North British was allowed a free hand in taking over another company in which the North Eastern had an interest, and the Edinburgh concern also gained running-powers from their own Border Counties line at Hexham over NER metals into Newcastle-upon-Tyne. This sinuous cross-Border route closed to passenger traffic in 1956, regarded as one of the most unremunerative lines ever built. Much of its trackbed is now under the waters of the Kielder Reservoir.

Historians appear mixed in their attitude towards this agreement. E.L. Ahrons declared that the North British had "sold their birthright for a mess of pottage" but the company's own historian, the late John Thomas, believed that the arrangement worked in everyone's favour. That the NBR officials would have been unlikely to agree with him is evidenced by their efforts to have the 1862 treaty rescinded, particularly around 1897.

In that year the Scottish company attempted to take over the running of all the East Coast trains north of Berwick, even although they had no

Portobello East junction in 1936, looking east. An East Coast express is coming over the junction with the Waverley Route (on the right) and has 3½ miles to go to Waverley. Engine power on display comprises a D20 4-4-0 piloting a C7 Atlantic. (W. E. Boyd collection)

track crossovers of their own to allow engine movements off up trains at the south end of the station, and the trains themselves were double-headed to keep time. It was a futile effort, doomed to failure despite being taken to arbitration – no fewer than eleven tribunals and two visits to the House of Lords – and the York-based company was able to make sinister threats about enforcing its theoretical running-powers throughout the NBR system. In 1898 the North Eastern even took to routing two Newcastle-Glasgow through passenger coaches per day via Carlisle, handing over there to the NB's hated rival, the Caledonian, in a unique example of East and West Coast concerns co-operating together against the interests of another company allied to one of them.

So it comes as no surprise to find that the running-powers wrangle was placed on a more legalistic footing by an agreement signed by the two companies on August 13th 1904 (effective from September 1st), whereby the NER could run up to four extra trains a day without notice on the NBR main-line between Berwick and Edinburgh, in addition to scheduled services.

This explains why the *Flying Scotsman* was being hauled into the heart of the Scottish capital by English locomotives at the turn of the century. It also underlines the strained atmosphere which existed between the two companies before agreement was reached. This came to a head in the autumn of 1900 when the NER announced that it would be accelerating the *Flying Scotsman* into Edinburgh by fifteen minutes, thus timetabling the journey for eight and a quarter hours. With the Edinburgh doocots well and truly a-flutter, the North British informed their supposed allies that they could not co-operate with these "working book extracts". Not only was the punctuality record of the train already poor over the previous winter – only 28 punctual arrivals in Edinburgh out of 102 – but there was always the danger of inciting another race with the West Coast. On October 12th 1896 both East and West Coast interests had agreed on a minimum 8¼ hour schedule for London-Edinburgh services during day-time, and it now looked as if the NER was intent on an acceleration which would breach this informal "treaty". No agreement was immediately reached in this 1900 skirmish, the result of which was the holding-up of the down *Scotsman* at Berwick-on-Tweed on November 1st.

Headed by S class 4-6-0 No 2010, the 275-ton express arrived at the Border town 1½ minutes early, having run from Newcastle in the very creditable time of 69½ minutes. However, this put it well ahead of its booked time, so the NB signalman refused to give it the road. "For 18½ minutes the NB officials held up the train" thundered no less an organ than *The Times* "while the officials enjoyed a chat on the squalid platforms, and the passengers fumed and made indignant remarks". Finally released, like a greyhound from a trap, 2010 tore up the line to Edinburgh, before experiencing an irritating series of signal delays, its arrival time at Waverley being one minute late by the unofficial timetable and fourteen minutes early by the public one.

Following this incident, there can be no better illustration of the deteriorating relationship between NB and NER than a press announce-ment in 1901 that the English company was seeking to establish its own booking-offices on North British stations between Berwick and Edin-burgh. The *Railway Magazine* reported that this "must further strain the cordiality of the relations existing on the East Coast route". While there is no evidence that such an installation took place, Edinburgh Waverley already accommodated such offices for both the North Eastern and the Midland. In 1898 both the GNR and NER had asked their Scottish ally to ensure that Waverley booking staff "would act with strict impartiality and not influence passengers to any route competing with the East Coast" (i.e. the Midland route to London through Carlisle).

The poor North British! Less than five years later it was subjected to a barrage of criticism from the Midland over the "preponderance" of East Coast posters at Waverley! The idea of a Midland employee painstakingly counting the East Coast posters at the station indicates the difficult relationship the Edinburgh company had with its English allies. On this occasion the NBR's Superintendent of the Line, David Deuchars, cannily explained that these advertisements were "provided and paid for by the

GNR and NER" and that the Midland could enjoy equal status "provided the Midland company supplied such boards at their own expense". To make matters worse, each English company suspected that the NBR might attempt to play one of them off against the other.

This suspicion may well account for the North Eastern's reaction to a crucial joint Midland-North British retimetabling in the summer of 1901 – although the records definitely show that this plan, which brought about the 1901 Race, was the Midland's idea.

On April 18th the NB Board of Directors heard "certain proposals of the Midland Railway Company with regard to the through train service by the Waverley Route between Scotland and England". These plans were already detailed enough to merit referral to a sub-committee, and Lord Dalkeith and Messrs Wieland and Howard were appointed to meet Midland directors with appropriate powers to conclude an agreement with them. Eight days later a slightly different line-up of NB directors met with Sir Ernest Paget, Lord Farrer, and two other Midland representatives in a top-level meeting at St Pancras.

At this conference the Midland expressed their desire to improve Anglo-Scottish services operated by the two companies. Farrer had already recommended to his own Board that trains to and from Scotland should stop not more than four times south of the Border, with a more stringent schedule being introduced. Perhaps all this was not before time; the previous year had seen the *Railway Magazine* asking

"why the English partner in this service
does not more fully second the endeavours of the NB
by expediting the trains south of Carlisle,
and so make the Waverley route a real competitor
with the East and West Coast services
between England and Scotland".

The Scottish directors, Messrs Wieland, Jackson, and Watson, entered into the spirit of the occasion by agreeing to accelerate the 09.30 out of St Pancras and its up counterpart, the 09.25. The details were left to be worked out at officer level.

York – ironically the headquarters of the North Eastern "enemy" – was the venue of the next meeting between the companies, on May 3rd. Here Deuchars, accompanied by Glen and Stevenson, met with Mugliston and Somers of the Midland, and confirmed a 135 minute non-stop schedule on the Waverley Route between Carlisle and Edinburgh, giving an 8 hr 35 minute schedule for the 406 mile journey over two very mountainous lines.

North of Carlisle the rake was to consist of five bogie vehicles, two of which were to run through to Aberdeen. The Midland suggested that this should be done by attaching them to the 18.40 out of Waverley – an apparently reasonable request since there should be up to 35 minutes available for the shunting required. But Deuchars was having none of it: the coaches would go forward on the 21.15, after a three-hour stand. He may have been worried by the logistics of incorporating yet another shunting operation into the complicated movements necessary at Waverley around the arrival time of three expresses from the south. The minutes of the meeting indicate Deuchars in a tough, unco-operative mood. He "could not entertain the question" of restaurant-car provision on one Waverley Route train, and made "strong objections" to various other ideas proposed.

Nevertheless, the NBR Superintendent was making a bold contribution to the new service. 135 minutes was a very fast schedule for a train on the 98¼ mile Waverley Route, with its two summits of Whitrope and Falahill around 900 feet above sea-level. It is believed that in 1889 a locomotive and saloon had negotiated the route in 105 minutes, a better documented run of 104 minutes, including a 9 minute signal stop, later being recorded in July 1916, but these did not include drawbar loads likely to test a locomotive. Even in the last days of the now-closed route, the 1960s, Class 45/46 diesels were taking 2½ hours or more for the journey, admittedly with five stops. Not that the exclusion of stops removed the difficulties for the 1901 footplate-crew, as we shall see later.

When the new timetable was published, showing an 18.05 arrival at Waverley for the express from St Pancras, there was a galvanic reaction from the North Eastern Railway. It immediately determined that the *Flying Scotsman* would now reach Edinburgh at 18.00 instead of 18.15, a breach of the 1896 understanding but one which the NER believed was justified in ensuring that the famous express would not risk delay from any late-running by the St Pancras train at Portobello. There was an obvious assumption – not entirely unjustified – that the Midland and North British would be unable to sustain their accelerated schedule over such a difficult route.

With the scene now set for two expresses from London due to approach Portobello East junction at a perilously similar time, a more detailed glance at the respective routes to Edinburgh is of interest, with some consideration given to the motive power available to the companies now readying themselves for the new timetable's introduction on July 1st.

NB VERSUS NE

The company most obviously relishing the possibility of a renewed Race to the North was the North Eastern. In 1901 it had no hesitation in accelerating through the terms of the 1896 agreement between East and West Coast companies for an 8¼ hour minimum limit on daytime trains between London and Edinburgh. Its decision to reach Edinburgh by 6 o'clock, and thus eclipse the Midland-NBR train which had left London half an hour earlier, was the action of a company very confident of the calibre of its machines and men.

This confidence was undoubtedly based on its new-found reputation for fast running. In 1888 and again in 1895, the NER had been second to none in its willingness to run for mile after mile at speed, often with an apparent disregard for safety. Ironically, one of the most notorious examples of this was the 81½mph, timed by none other than the great railway journalist Charles Rous-Martin, over a 15 mph speed restriction at Portobello, in North British territory!

The already highly-regarded stud of the North Eastern M class 4-4-0 engines, which had made such a name for itself six years before, had been succeeded, first by larger 4-4-0s of the R class, and then by class S 4-6-0s, one of which already had shown its capabilities in the November 1900 incident. The latter class comprised the first locomotives of their wheel-arrangement designed for express passenger traffic, although their arrival was not to be as influential as the 4-6-0 configuration on the Great Western engine scene.

The East Coast line was soon to see the introduction of a fleet of

9

Atlantic (4-4-2) classes in all three of the constituent companies. The first of these was already in service, but not north of York. The only NER locomotive specified in contemporary reports in 1901 was in fact one of the R class 4-4-0s.

The North Eastern's southern ally, the Great Northern, will not be considered here as, alone among the traditional rivals, there is no contemporary evidence that it altered its attitudes or working practices to beat the St Pancras departure into Edinburgh, beyond a token two minute early handover to the NER at York. Apart from this, all time-gaining on the East Coast side appears to have happened north of York. At that time, the GNR was in the throes of a fascinating transition from single-wheel express locomotives to a fleet of 4-4-0s and the new Atlantics. Examples of the latter may have been used on the *Flying Scotsman*, although a contemporary photograph records a 1328 class 4-4-0 on the named express at around this time.

What of the East Coast racetrack, the line from Newcastle to Edinburgh? It lacked the major adverse gradients which so hindered the NER's opponents; indeed the steepest gradient to be encountered faced southbound trains – Cockburnspath bank. Down trains had to tackle Longhoughton bank – five miles at l70, but this was scarcely of Beattock or Whitrope severity. The most difficult climb for northbound trains was that to Grantshouse (summit of Cockburnspath), of which the seasoned traveller W.J. Scott said "The dead slow for Berwick station makes the four miles' rise at 190 from that point a very hard one". While the *Flying Scotsman* was not booked to stop at the Border town in l90l, the cramped layout of the station, not rebuilt until LNER days, made trains slow down to almost walking pace anyway. The steepest incline on the line – and one facing northbound trains – does not count for comparative purposes as the 1¼ mile climb at 1 in 78 from St Margaret's to Waverley had to be surmounted by the expresses from both King's Cross and St Pancras. In any event, NER locomotive No 1621 was recorded near the top of the St Margaret's climb doing 64 mph in l895, which, considering the nearness of the Waverley platforms, was perhaps a little too exciting to bear repeating!

It is ironic that the Midland and the North British, unconscious instigators of the accelerations of 1901, should have the most difficult task of all in carrying out their new timetables. Their route north of Leeds was by the Settle and Carlisle line presently threatened with closure, and from the Border City to the Scottish capital via the Waverley Route, closed in 1969.

Anyone with any knowledge of the British railway system will need no telling that these were two of the most demanding express passenger routes in the country. Indeed, their present-day removal from the modern Inter-City network underlines the difficulties involved in operating them, not assisted by the paucity of intermediate traffic they generated. While the Settle and Carlisle is still open to some passenger traffic, and its long gradients at 1 in 100 still offer an operating difficulty even to modern diesel traction, its future is uncertain. In operating terms, its 113 mile length from Leeds to Carlisle, including a summit of 1169 feet at Aisgill, was a formidable challenge to a hand-fuelled steam locomotive scheduled to make such a journey in less than 2 hours 20 minutes.

Not for nothing is the route known as "The long drag"! To reach Aisgill Summit long spells of hard climbing are necessary from both north and south. For northbound trains the climb begins at Settle Junction, about three and a half miles north of Hellifield. This continues, mainly at 1 in 100, up to Blea Moor tunnel some fourteen miles away. Thereafter there is a plateau of almost level track until the summit is reached, where begins a descent almost exactly a counterpart to the climb from the south. Despite all this, the Settle and Carlisle provided opportunities for fast running if the engine was able and the crew were willing. The lack of sharp curves and the even gradation allowed a run to be "paced", and high speeds could be attained on the straight downhill stretches.

The records show that, probably uniquely in the 1901 contest, the Midland employed "single" locomotives, designed by S.W. Johnson, on the southern part of its route. The term "single" means that the engine's tractive effort was concentrated on a single pair of driving wheels, usually of considerable diameter, as thirteen years earlier with the Caledonian's No 123. It was very much an 1870s concept, and such engines were regarded as likely to slip easily, although there is no record of any appreciable time being lost by single-wheelers running the Anglo-Scottish expresses during this period. Their continued use into the twentieth century is a source for some wonder.

According to figures published by the Railway Correspondence and Travel Society, an express in 1880 was likely to seat 248 passengers in a rake of vehicles totalling 116 tons. Within sixteen years, more than double that tare weight would be required to accommodate a mere four passengers extra (237 tons for 252 passengers)! The Midland was no exception to this trend for heavier, more comfortable and better equipped trains. Indeed, one traveller described the Midland and North British Joint stock on the St Pancras – Waverley service in 1901 as "brilliantly handsome". Dual-fitted with vacuum and Westinghouse brakes (the latter for use on the NBR, which did not begin fitting vacuum brakes on its coaching stock for another ten years), these coaches were built at Derby and paid for by both companies on a ratio calculated on a mileage basis. The reported cost apportionment which saw the Midland paying twice the Scottish company's share would appear to favour Derby; a true ratio based on respective mileages would surely have been 3:1, unless mileage north of Edinburgh was being taken into account.

The Midland's "singles" would be required to haul a load some seventy tons heavier than the 1880 average. The only locomotive of this type reported to have operated one of the 1901 trains was No 1853, one of the 1889 batch of 7½ foot single-wheelers nicknamed "spinners".

North of Leeds, and in complete contrast, a 4-4-0 express locomotive of comparatively massive proportions had just been introduced on the Settle-Carlisle line. Yet it was also a Johnson-designed engine. The 2606 class, later renumbered as the 700s, were fitted with Belpaire fireboxes giving them a powerful appearance, and their performance did not belie it. These were simple (i.e. non-compound) locomotives, and were soon to be superseded by the same designer's compound 4-4-0s which eventually (and probably anachronistically) became the standard express passenger design for the London Midland and Scottish Railway in the first half of the 1920s. So the 2606s did not make the impact they perhaps deserved – although nearly two dozen survived through to nationalisation in 1948 and their work is certainly worth recording.

But if there is an old truism that "the willing horse always gets the hardest road", there would have had to be plenty of willing steeds in the North British stable. So badly handicapped was the Waverley Route as a main-line that it scarcely merited such a description at all.

Involving climbs to two summits of around 900 feet, the line suffered from having been constructed piecemeal. While the Caledonian line between Carlisle and Edinburgh was the result of a visionary concept to link the Border City – and points south – with Glasgow, Edinburgh, and the north of Scotland, allowing fast running downhill, the Waverley Route had inched south from the Edinburgh area as part of the former Edinburgh and Dalkeith Railway (effectively a local waggonway) connecting the Scottish capital with the Lothian coalfield. It then became the North British's main branch to Hawick in 1849, only extended to Carlisle some thirteen years later. At that time there was no Midland presence at the Border City, so the NBR line was built more as a cross-country route rather than as an Anglo-Scottish main-line.

If it seems incongruous that northbound trains from London could be considered to be racing when one had started off no less than half an hour earlier than the other, the Waverley Route provided a perfect natural "handicap". From Carlisle there was a virtual reverse bend before the River Eden was crossed for the second time in less than a mile. Although the Debateable Lands of the Border were comparatively flat, ten miles of almost unceasing climb had then to be accomplished to Whitrope Summit at an average gradient of around 1 in 80. From there downhill to Hawick, numerous bends prevented high speed running, while on the comparatively flat stretch between Hawick and Galashiels there was an awkward mini-summit at Standhill to be climbed at grades of 1 in 150/200. North of Galashiels there was a gradual, but unrelenting climb to Falahill, the line's second summit of around 900 feet, but even downhill from here on the last eighteen miles to Edinburgh the route's curvature made speeds of more than a mile a minute appear almost reckless.

Although running through beautiful but often barren scenery, the erstwhile Waverley Route also had an industrial character at its northern end, as this picture at Fushiebridge testifies. A2 Pacific No. 60528 Tudor Minstrel *lifts a heavy King's Cross express up Falahill bank at a time in 1948 when trains from the East Coast main-line were diverted over the Waverley Route and then along the St. Boswells-Tweedmouth line. A colliery line reached Fushiebridge from the north-east, as can be guessed from the right background of the photograph, but there was also an industrial line trailing in from the south-west where an Andes-style graded incline is still visible to the eye, evidence of a lime-working which once had no fewer than three different gauges operating. (J. Robertson)*

Twelve years before the 1901 episode made headlines, the much-travelled railway author W.M. Acworth had commended the standard of Waverley Route running by the NBR. In his book *The Railways of Scotland*, he asks;

> "What the *Chemin de fer du Nord* authorities, who cannot manage to keep time with their expresses from Paris to Amiens at some 40mph, would think of hauling over this road the heavy Pullmans of the Midland down Highland expresses, in 140 minutes without a stop, one really would like to know. Probably they would think what a nuisance competition was ..."

"Competition" was certainly the right word for what motivated the protagonists of 1901, when the schedule was even tougher, and how pleasant to see this Scottish railway being so favourably viewed in a European context!

Like the other railway companies involved in 1901, the North British had a fleet of 4-4-0 locomotives for express passenger traffic. These were members of the M class, built in two "marks" as the 476 and 729 sub-classes by Matthew Holmes. As early as 1897 a press photograph of No 729 was captioned with the comment "Ready to try conclusions with the enlarged (Caledonian) Dunalastairs"!

The only NBR engine specified in the documents concerning the 1901 Race was one of the 729 series. With 6 feet 6 inch driving wheels, these locomotives later became LNER class D31, and many of them including 738 – the only NBR engine to be identified by the *Scotsman* newspaper in the 1901 incident – ended their days on the Great North of Scotland section where it was finally withdrawn in 1939. The most significant statistic about these interesting though unexceptional engines was the fact that their tenders held 3,500 gallons of water. Running non-stop on the Waverley Route, they would need every drop.

The provision of water-troughs was crucially important. In 1860 the London and North Western had pioneered these innovatory facilities at Mochdre on the Chester-Holyhead line, enabling a steam locomotive to pick up thousands of gallons of water from troughs between the running rails while travelling at speed.

Troughs were now in commission on the East Coast line, and north of Newcastle the North Eastern engines picked up at Lucker, near Belford, laid some three years previously. This left the Midland and North British to do the real heroics – there were no troughs on the Settle and Carlisle line until 1907 when the country's highest set of troughs were laid at Dent. North of Carlisle, it would not be too cynical to say that there were hardly any stretches of straight line long enough, or curves of a gentle enough radius, on the Waverley Route to accommodate troughs, except possibly immediately north of Melrose. Even here there was a 1:200 gradient, making their installation impracticable. But there is no evidence that the NBR ever seriously considered their installation, and it remained one of the largest railway companies not to instal water-troughs.

A1 on the Waverley Route. Another East Coast express is seen on a diversion through the central Borders, this time in 1950. The locomotive is A1 Pacific No. 60126, named Sir Vincent Raven *later that year, and seen here heading a down named express on Falahill bank. (J. Robertson)*

COCKING THE PISTOL

It is an indication of how the public — and the media — were antici-
pating another Railway Race, that a large crowd turned out on Monday
July 1st 1901 to see the new 09.25 leave Waverley for St Pancras. Trains
may always have raced *to* the North, according to the London-orientated
media and historians, but there was plenty of interest in the northern
capital too should there ever be a Railway Race to the South!

The Scotsman newspaper was to despatch a journalist to the Waverley
every evening to see the London expresses arrive, but exceeded even this
on Monday 1st. Their correspondent, unfortunately anonymous, travelled
with the southbound train as far as Carlisle and returned on the
corresponding down journey, providing one highly detailed log which is
reproduced at the rear of this book.

The scene at the platform end at Waverley station must have been a
colourful one that breezy July morning – Holmes 4-4-0 No 738 stood at the
head of a sumptuous rake of Midland & North British joint stock. Even so,
although making a brave sight, 738 may have disappointed some
observers, who, according to *The Scotsman,* had come hoping to witness
the train's departure behind one of the powerful new Midland 4-4-0s. This
was based on the obvious misconception that the Midland may have
enjoyed the same running-powers over the Waverley Route that the North
Eastern had north of Berwick. The North British would make no excuses
for disappointing them. If there was going to be another race, the NBR
could provide its own motive power!

Falahill signal-box on the Up side of the Waverley Route, approximately eighteen miles from Edinburgh, at a height of about 900 feet above sea-level. From here the NBR racer could run downhill as fast as the curves and pitslacks would allow to Portobello East junction. (W. E. Boyd collection)

Surrounded by a large crowd, 738 was in the charge of a crew supervised by Inspector Brown, with Mr Wilson of the Superintendent of the Line's office also present. Only twenty-seven passengers were conveyed by the express, pulling out on what *The Scotsman* called its "maiden journey". Twelve of them were bound for London, ten more than travelled south to the capital on the 14.10 out of Waverley later that day, and this underlines the uneconomic nature of many of the Edinburgh-London services by this route. Not many years were to pass before the North British was to request from the Midland — and receive — financial subsidies for their share in operating these Anglo-Scottish trains.

Despite almost gale-force winds, 738 started off the new accelerated service with a fine run to Carlisle. Gorebridge, twelve miles out at the foot of the worst part of the climb to Falahill, was passed in 21 minutes, Tynehead four miles farther on, in twenty-nine. The summit of the bank, every bit as challenging as Beattock, was surmounted at 30 mph in 32½ minutes for the eighteen miles. This was an excellent effort for a crew who could never allow the problem of water consumption to escape their attention. Down the other side of the bank, successive miles were reeled off at 42, 45, 52, 55, and 56 mph, with the next 8¾ miles to Stow taking only ten minutes. If this does not sound particularly impressive, a traveller on the modern A7 will see the way that the now-closed Waverley Route trackbed threads its way down the valley of the Gala Water, crossing and re-crossing the river on eight bridges in a succession of speed-restricting bends between Stow and Galashiels.

No passing time was recorded for the latter, a major Border town, but we know that Hawick (52¾ miles) was negotiated at 30 mph in 74 minutes. Immediately, the climb to Whitrope began, up the windswept valley of the Slitrig Water, with 738's exhaust no doubt raising the pheasants and whaups. Only twenty-two minutes were occupied to passing Riccarton Junction, where the unremunerative Hexham line gave the North British the worthless prize of entry to Newcastle by the back-door, but by this time Whitrope summit was behind 738, and she could now run as fast as the curves allowed. 56, 60, 58, 58, 59, 58, 58, 56, 60, 60, 57, were the successive speeds recorded – a superbly consistent performance, but one which only just gave a ½ minute early arrival at Carlisle. Possibly delayed by signals, 738 ground her way round the Caldew curve at a mere ten mph, before bringing her train into the Citadel station.

"Considering the gale in the hills and the various slacks, this was good running" opined *The Scotsman*, "and the large crowd of officials of the (other) seven companies who use the joint station at Carlisle heartily congratulated the NB men on their excellent work". As one of the other companies operating out of Carlisle was the North Eastern, it is pleasant to record this sporting gesture from a rival, for 738 would be powering the down train some 4½ hours later, after servicing at Canal depot.

Just before turning our attention to the northbound train, already on its way north of Leicester, there is just time to notice that the Midland made up the 09.25 southbound with a through connection from Glasgow. This arrived from the Glasgow South Western system seventeen minutes late, headed by what *The Scotsman* sniffily described as a "diminutive old loco", and eventual arrival at St Pancras was no less than 29 minutes behind time. 738's efforts had been for naught – so far.

At this very moment, some two hundred miles to the south, the 09.30 northbound was well on its way, approaching Loughborough. This was the real racer, the train considered as the rival to the East Coast's *Flying Scotsman*. Its complement of passengers included Lord Farrer, the architect of the Midland accelerations, and the Rev. W.J. Scott, an amateur, although highly-respected, railway journalist.

Ten years after the Race to Scotland, a Midland Railway "Single" is photographed at Harefield in Gloucestershire on a Bradford-Bristol express. This was No. 614, one of the class of forty-two such engines which were renumbered by the Midland after 1901, around the time when the first of the famous Compound 4-4-0s were introduced and which revolutionised that company's motive power policy. (Scottish Record Office)

The 09.30's start was some thirty seconds behind time, but otherwise the Midland had begun well. Headed by a Johnson locomotive with single driving wheels of 7½ feet diameter, the train gained three minutes on its non-stop dash to Leicester. Here the Johnson "single" was replaced, and modern readers can only regret – not for the last time – the reverend gentleman's casual attitude to identifying locomotives. Mr Scott's writings specify the locomotive on the St Pancras – Leicester section only as being "one of the 1853 class". Yet, according to the confusing Midland numbering of the time, if the engine was not number 1853 itself, but was within the sequence 1854-61, it would have been one of the 7 foot 4 inch "spinners". 1853, with driving wheels of two inches greater diameter, was turned out in 1889 and won a gold medal at a trade fair in Paris that year.

Whatever its identity, this was the only single participating in the 1901 episode, and at Leicester was replaced by a 7 ft 4-4-0 of the "60" class from the same designer. Unaccountably, the three-minute early arrival was converted into a departure five minutes behind time, and this was the beginning of a troublesome leg of the run.

Through the Midlands the 09.30 experienced serious delays, and the

19

railway enthusiasts on board must have despaired of their train offering the *Flying Scotsman* serious competition. There was a slowing for a new bridge being built at Alfreton, and slacks at Swinton and Cudworth. At Chesterfield the train filled up with passengers from Birmingham travelling to Leeds for an onward journey to Scarborough – they may not even have been aware they were travelling on a "racer". Certainly by Leeds, the 09.30 was no less than fourteen minutes behind time. The next part of the route was over the Settle and Carlisle line – not one where time could easily be made up. But in fact it was, thanks to the latest 4-4-0 class from Johnson's drawing-board.

The "2606" locomotives were already setting records over the hilly route to Carlisle, and although Mr Scott failed to record speeds, some impressive work was done over the next 112 miles with this 188 ton load. Two minutes were regained by Settle, despite a slow passage through the junction at Hellifield, but speed on the climb to Blea Moor was understandably low. No water-troughs existed on this line at the time, and this may account for the cautious driving, even after the worst of the climbing was over. After spending 26 minutes on the 17 miles from Hellifield to Blea Moor, the 4-4-0 was eased on the eight mile stretch from there to Hawes Junction, taking 11¼ minutes, an average of only 42½ mph. (See Appendix B).

Matters certainly improved from then on! Speed built up on the level to Aisgill and the falling gradient thereafter — the 21¼ miles from Hawes Junction to Appleby being covered in 19 minutes. Lazonby, nearly 15¼ miles farther on, was passed 13 minutes later, and Carlisle reached at 15.51, only six minutes behind time. Without checks, the Midland 4-4-0 so cryptically described by Scott as "a coupled engine" had reeled off the last 30¼ miles in almost exactly thirty minutes, halving the time-deficit. In his book *Main Lines Across the Border*, O.S. Nock records a 1902 run by one of these "Belpaire" engines running the 48½ miles from Aisgill to Carlisle, start to stop, in the remarkable time of five seconds less than 42 minutes (as opposed to Scott's approximate timing of 45 minutes pass to stop). However, the engine in 1902 had enjoyed the benefit of a pilot engine up "the long drag" and there would have been reserves of steam and fuel for the crew to call upon. Whatever the merits of this run in July 1901, it was more exceptional than commonplace.

At Carlisle, Crimson Lake gave way to Gamboge. The lovingly-applied Midland livery was one of the eight colour schemes seen on locomotives working in and out of the Citadel station, and was arguably the most distinguished of them all. The North British engine, with its enigmatic hue of greenish-brown, sometimes rendered as a mustard shade at various times, was waiting to take the train forward to the Scottish capital.

This changeover was no easy matter. Two coaches for Glasgow had to be detached for onward transit over the Glasgow South Western system to

20

their St Enoch terminus. The idea was to form two separate trains for the north at the same platform, the dark-green GSWR engines reversing by way of points half way down the platform on to the Glasgow vehicles drawn off the back of the Edinburgh section.

Meanwhile the NB locomotive was being coupled to the front of the train and the crews hurriedly changing the braking system from vacuum – used by the Midland – to Westinghouse. That this inevitably required more than the allotted five minutes, can be seen from the figures in the appendix for time-keeping on the 09.30. During the race period between the 1st and 8th of July inclusive, an average of three and a half minutes were lost in the Citadel every day; indeed there was only one occasion when the changeover was accomplished within schedule during the first thirteen attempts. This inaugural journey was no exception to the trend, and the time dropped here varied between one minute and three, according to conflicting reports.

So, nine minutes late, NBR number 738 steamed north from Carlisle on her quest to beat the North Eastern to Edinburgh. With the rake reduced to five vehicles comprising a van, composite, third class, dining car, and composite brake, 150 tons gross, the train took the turn-off for the Waverley Route. "Excellent work at once began" commented *The Scotsman*. Longtown (9½ miles) was passed in only 12¼ minutes, and Riddings (14¼ miles) taken at 62 mph in 17½ minutes. The next 18¼ miles to Riccarton were nearly all uphill and understandably occupied 27½ minutes, with the driver not wishing to risk using too much water or tire his fireman with two-thirds of the run still to go.

After topping Whitrope, 738 dived into the tunnel, her immediate climb over. Speed was not allowed to exceed 61 mph on the sharp bends downhill to Hawick, 45½ miles accomplished in 62 minutes. On the comparatively easier section to Galashiels mile-a-minute rates were recorded at St Boswells and Melrose, the 19¼ miles being run in 21½ minutes. "Here it was realised," reported the newspaper, "that the train was making a very fine run, and hopes rose that Edinburgh might be reached in time". Galashiels was passed slowly and the climb to Falahill began.

Up the valley of the Gala Water went the 09.30, her progress being recorded and timed by a least two of her passengers. Falahill summit was attained in 105 minutes from Carlisle, and her driver then gave 738 her head as she stormed towards Edinburgh. Despite the curves and mining slacks, 55 mph was averaged downhill towards Portobello. Would she beat the North Eastern? Was a punctual arrival possible after a nine minute late start from Carlisle on an unprecedentedly fast schedule?

Niddrie North signals were "off" – she was cleared through Portobello East! 738 brought her train on to the East Coast main-line with no sign of a train signalled from the Berwick direction. After a journey of more than four hundred miles, the 09.30 was on the last lap of the race.

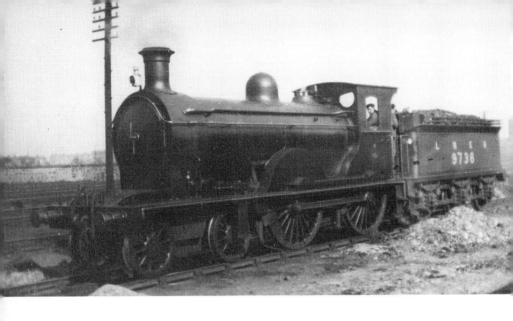

Rebuilt with enclosed cab, a luxury not available to the footplatemen of 1901, NBR 738 was renumbered as 9738 when photographed simmering at Craigentinny in 1926. Reclassified as a D31, this veteran of the 1901 incident, in which she ran non-stop from Carlisle to Edinburgh in 126 minutes over the Waverley Route, was later transferred to the GNSR section where she worked until withdrawal in 1939. (W. E. Boyd collection)

NER Class R 4-4-0 No. 2015 photographed passing Craigentinny, in Edinburgh's eastern suburbs, on an Edinburgh-bound stopping train in 1926, twenty-five years after the Race in which she was so prominent. (W. E. Boyd collection)

WINNING IS ALL

With all brakes jammed on, 738 and her train shot from the Calton tunnel into the Waverley station — and found that they had lost.

An appreciative crowd was already clustered round the North Eastern R class 4-4-0 No 2015 which had brought in the *Flying Scotsman* four minutes previously, thirteen minutes ahead of the published schedule. The excited onlookers were probably unaware that the NER's intention to reach Edinburgh by six o'clock was no secret amongst the railway companies. As far as the crowds were concerned – and they included such local illuminati as the Lord Justice Clerk of Scotland on the platform – there seemed to be a race developing to be first to Edinburgh with the morning departures from London.

Nor was the Scottish capital alone in viewing developments with such excitement. *The Newcastle Evening Chronicle* reported that both portions of the 10.00 ex-King's Cross were seen off from Newcastle by large crowds, and there was considerable satisfaction with the North Eastern's performance that day. It appears that the 124½ miles on the Newcastle-Edinburgh section was run in 147 minutes – a time which O.S. Nock later described as "not anything very wonderful". By 1895 standards it was not, although a signal check at Tweedmouth should be taken into account. *The Scotsman* reported that the express was held at Tweedmouth for six minutes, while another report mentions a seven minute delay. It seems reasonable to assume that the NBR arrested the train's progress intentionally, just as they had done the previous November, and as we shall see, as they were to do again before the racing episode of July 1901 was over.

So began the third railway race to the North. On Tuesday July 2nd, the Midland brought their train into Carlisle twenty minutes down due to "the weather in England being against the making of good time". (Official NBR statistics gave the Carlisle *departure* time as being twenty-one minutes late). Nevertheless, the NBR again did well north of Carlisle by knocking seven minutes (eight according to the NBR) off the arrears accumulated south of the Border. Despite this effort, the Scottish company did not even glimpse the North Eastern's tail-lamp on the approach to Edinburgh. The King's Cross train was into Waverley fifteen minutes before it, after gaining some twelve minutes on schedule after a punctual departure from Newcastle, eleven of these reportedly having been gained south of Berwick. (The "bad weather" must have been peculiar to the Settle-Carlisle line!) Again, one wonders if the NB signalmen were doing their worst to impede the *Flying Scotsman*, considering that the time-gain north of the Border did not match that of the Newcastle-Berwick section.

The Wednesday saw the NER's winning margin down to only six minutes, despite the North British apparently gaining five minutes on arrears between Galashiels and Edinburgh alone – a considerable effort that must pass unconfirmed – but on the 4th there was no contest. With the Midland forced to make an emergency stop for water at Blea Moor, Carlisle was reached sixteen minutes late. The inevitable delay in changing brake systems meant that the NBR engine's feat in bringing the train into Waverley only fourteen minutes behind time was commendable.

Nor did the running over the Waverley Route escape the attention of the press. The *Carlisle Patriot* commented on July 5th:

> "The feature of the running of the week has been the excellent work of the NB between Carlisle and Edinburgh; it not only has kept up to time as a rule – but on more than one occasion it made up from seven to twelve minutes which its ally lost south of Carlisle."

"The Midland is hopelessly out of the hunt". That was the scathing opinion of the *Railway Times*, which went on:

> "Instead of wasting energy and money in running 'racing' trains, it looks as if the shareholders' interests would be much better served by a mutual agreement to restrict the services to the traffic requirements, and, if possible, to 'pool' the receipts. The shareholders ... are certainly in no mood to see their greatly diminished profits frittered away in competitions of this character".

25

Despite sustained efforts by the North British, the North Eastern was the winner on the first four days of competition. But that was not the case on Friday July 5th. On that day a new competitor emerged, or more accurately, there re-emerged a runner whom the bystanders had quite forgotten.

At twenty minutes to six on that summer evening, Caledonian "Dunalastair" 4-4-0 No. 899 brought the 10.00 ex-Euston into Edinburgh's Princes Street station. This was no less than thirty-five minutes ahead of schedule, and only two minutes slower than the West Coast record time in 1888.

Platforms almost empty of onlookers were 899's reward. Only a few company officials were aware of the train's progress, and most railway enthusiasts were at Waverley, a mile away at the other end of the capital's Princes Street. The station of that name was to close in 1965, so the finishing-post for this West Coast racer exists now only in the realms of history.

According to the local paper, LNWR and CR train-crews had been under specific orders all week not to reach Edinburgh before time with the 10 o'clock:

> "The Caledonian and the North Western com-
> panies resolved at the beginning of the week to
> await developments, the engine-drivers and
> guards on the London trains being instructed to
> the effect that in no account were the trains to run
> faster than permitted by the companies' time-
> tables. When, however, it became apparent the
> East Coast companies were running their *Flying
> Scotsman* ahead of schedule time, the West
> Coast companies determined to show the public
> what they in turn could do".

The West Coast companies, not involved imminently in the outbreak of racing in 1901, had a difficult route to operate, compared to the East Coast. Shap and Beattock, south and north of Carlisle respectively, were notorious natural barriers to swift progress. The former necessitated five miles of climbing at 1 in 75; Beattock was twice as long and just as steep. Had the race been to Glasgow those would have been the only major summits to overcome. However, after a slow start from Carstairs junction Edinburgh-wards, the Caledonian trains were faced with Cobbinshaw summit, another ten miles of hard climbing up to the 880 feet contour.

Since 1896 the Caledonian had been equipping itself with a superb stable of "Dunalastair" class 4-4-0s, the latest "mark" being known as the

Interior of Princes Street station looking north-eastwards from the widest of the seven platforms (1/2), in 1928 with the road entrance/exit out of sight in the left background. A pile of destination boards in the foreground appears to include a board for one of the named London expresses, possibly the Edinburgh section of the "Royal Scot". (Scottish Record Office)

"Dunalastair IIIs" or 900s. These were introduced in the summer of 1900 and so highly-regarded were these machines that the *Railway Magazine* of that year, in describing that year's schedules as "dull", went on to commiserate with the "magnificent 900s ... blowing their safety valves off with impatience." In fact at least one "III" thoroughly distinguished itself by making probably the finest run of the entire 1901 conflict, as will soon be examined in as much detail as history will allow. Unfortunately, O.S. Nock, points out in his book *The Caledonian Dunalastairs and associated classes* "not many detailed timings of the 'Dunalastair III' class in their early days have been passed down to us today" – something modern readers can only regret. Suffice to say that, hard road or not, the Caledonian was ready for anything.

In some ways the London and North Western Railway's engine fleet was the most interesting of all, but because it has been well-documented by W.A. Tuplin (*North Western Steam*) and by O.S. Nock (*Premier Line*), it is not intended to deal with these locomotives in detail. On a railway where there was considerable experiment with compounding, the North Western shunned its new "Jubilee" and "Black Prince" classes of 4-4-0s when the race heated up and turned to its beloved "Jumbos". These were the only engines in the 1901 Race not fitted with a leading bogie, and in some cases were effectively forty years old. Unfortunately, as we shall see, the secretive suddenness of the West Coast's entry into the conflict means that the performance of these little engines in 1901 has not been properly documented.

No matter the small size of their locomotive tenders, the West Coast had no water replenishment problems south of Carlisle, thanks to the LNWR's pioneering of water-troughs, but from there to Edinburgh the Caledonian had no such facilities. However, the eight-wheel tenders of the new "Dunalastair IIIs" held 4,500 gallons of water, and the Caledonian's chairman, Sir James Thomson, was justified in telling a journalist some years earlier that this class was capable of long journeys without stopping for water replenishment.

In fact, the West Coast train had arrived at Edinburgh late on the first three days of the week when the East Coast rivals were racing for Portobello East. But the arrival time at Princes Street was improving all that week, the Friday arrival being no less than 54 minutes better than the Monday's. It was reported that the NER's ignoring of the published timetable had spurred the West Coast into action, although the newspapers' habit of reporting Princes Street arrival times – whether the West Coast considered itself to be racing or not – had triggered a response from the authorities in Crewe and Glasgow.

The North Western started the ball rolling on July 5th by running the 290-ton train, almost certainly double-headed, ahead of booked time. By Rugby two minutes had been gained on schedule and another five by Crewe. Here the train was split, with the Edinburgh portion going on ahead. This 150-ton load was brought into Carlisle no less than fourteen minutes early by one of the LNWR "Precedent" class 2-4-0s. These were based on the Ramsbottom "Newton" class of the 1860s and could reasonably claim to be the oldest locomotives – or at least those of the oldest design – in the 1901 episode. We know that 1572 *Gladstone* had been responsible for the train on unspecified dates in early July, on one occasion bringing a 140-ton load over the 141 miles from Crewe, inclusive of Shap and a five minute signal holdup, in 161½ minutes, with a deliberately slow approach to the Border City to avoid an early arrival, according to a

Newton class 2-4-0 of the London and North Western Railway, pictured at Carlisle (Upperby) in 1926. These locomotives were developments of a Ramsbottom 1860s design, colloquially known as "Jumbos", and featured in all the racing involving the West Coast companies. (W. E. Boyd collection)

report in the technical press. The fine run on July 5th has the hallmark of *Gladstone* haulage.

Black gave way to Prussian Blue in another of Carlisle's colour changes and the 10.00 headed north, without waiting for booked time, behind Caledonian 4-4-0 number 899. This eighteen-month old locomotive was based at Dalry Road, a now-vanished depot in Edinburgh, so she had her nose towards the stable as she tore northwards.

Unfortunately, we have no detailed timings of what must have been a remarkable run, accomplished in only 108 minutes for the 100½ miles inclusive of summits at Beattock and Cobbinshaw. According to both *The Scotsman* and the *Glasgow Herald*, confirmed by the *Railway Magazine*, the express suffered two signal checks on Beattock bank, lasting a total of eight minutes. A worse place to have to restart after being delayed can hardly be imagined! Assuming a slow passage at Summit, it would appear that the notorious bank could not have been climbed in less than twenty-four minutes, ten more than the Caledonian "Single" No 123 which was timed storming the ten miles of Beattock bank in less than fourteen minutes in August 1888. If 123's performance is regarded as a maximum theoretically attainable by 899, a nett time for the run between

Carlisle and Edinburgh (Princes Street) of less than 100 minutes is almost certain, and 95 minutes was later suggested by the Reverend Scott. This is probably a little too low, given that some standing time at Carlisle was cut. But it is impossible to deny that 899 made a sparkling contribution to the 1901 Race.

899's work was soon to be discussed on the floor of the House of Commons, an M.P. named Bell asking the President of the Board of Trade on July 11th if "he would take steps, by legislation or otherwise, to prevent a continuation of such practice". His question, directed towards the possible dangers inherent in railway racing, attracted a non-committal reply. The railways were responsible for passenger safety, he was told.

While 899 was simmering at the Princes Street buffer-stops on that Friday evening, the North Eastern was still some twenty-nine minutes south of Waverley, three minutes ahead of the North British. Whether the East Coast felt threatened by this whiff of 1888 grapeshot is still a matter for debate. Two contemporary observers believed that there was no East Coast response at all – the Reverend Scott maintaining curiously that the West Coast run was unworthy of reply. Nevertheless, it is arguable that the North Eastern responded by bringing the overnight 20.15 ex-King's Cross into Waverley on the morning of Saturday 6th nine minutes early, in 7 hours 36 minutes. This was actually four minutes faster than the West Coast effort, and a more obvious reply can hardly be imagined. In passing, it seems strange that the overnight Anglo-Scottish services should be faster than the day trains, something which could hardly have impressed the travelling public.

If this was a potential flashpoint in the 1901 Race, it was not well-timed. The Saturday, with all its excursion traffic, now made its demands on the companies. Twelve hundred extra passengers alighted from special trains at Waverley, while two thousand entrained for Kirkcaldy and five hundred for Dalkeith. Princes Street had six hundred extra passengers arriving, and some four times as many departed for Lanark, Cramond (Barnton), and Balerno. All this indicates the volume of special traffic moving on the rail network as the three Edinburgh expresses sped northwards.

The North Eastern was in by six minutes past six, having gained nine minutes from Berwick, but the NBR was nine minutes later, fully ten minutes behind time, despite the gain of a minute from Carlisle. Meanwhile, the Caledonian had contented itself with an arrival at Princes Street only seventeen minutes ahead of time!

So far, the Midland and North British had not succeeded in reaching Edinburgh on time once, nor had they beaten their racing rival, the North Eastern. However, their fortunes were to change on Monday 8th.

How are the mighty fallen! Difficult to believe that this forlorn machine, photographed at Dalry Road shed in August 1933, made the fastest-known steam-hauled run between Carlisle and Edinburgh (in nett terms). Caledonian "Dunalastair III" 4-4-0 No. 899 is shown, in rebuilt state as LMS No. 14348, complete with double-bogie tender which facilitated non-stop running over long stretches of the Caledonian main-line. (Scottish Record Office)

Veteran of the 1888 Race to Edinburgh, Caledonian 4-2-2 No. 123 stands at Slateford with preserved CR coaches in March 1955. Her best time between Carlisle and Edinburgh was not quite equalled in 1901, thanks to signal delays. (W. S. Sellar)

THE CONCLUSION

There seems no pressing reason why Monday July 8th should have been the final day of the 1901 Race. Certainly, the specialised railway press was howling for an end to such reckless behaviour, *Herapath's Railway Journal* and the other magazines aimed at the railway stockholder arguing that, far from competing for Anglo-Scottish traffic, the six companies should be pooling it to avoid unnecessary expense. Writing in *The Engineer*, that doyen of railway writers, Charles Rous-Martin, announced on July 5th that there was no race to Edinburgh at all, and that the real competition was between the Midland and Great Northern for London-Leeds traffic. Of course, his opinion was published on the day of the West Coast's exceptional run, marking their entry into the non-existent race!

There was certainly a noticeable slackening of effort by the West Coast companies by the 8th, confirming the theory that their work three days earlier was intended solely as a reminder of what they could do.

On this Monday, *Gladstone* was replaced by sister-engine No 1621 *Talavera* on the Crew-Carlisle section of the West Coast main-line. No detailed timings have been recorded, although we know that arrival at Carlisle was some twelve minutes early. In contrast to the previous Friday it seems that the Caledonian waited for "time" before setting off for the north, and there was the exciting possibility of *two* racing trains standing in the through platforms at Citadel at the same time, if only for a few

33

seconds. As it was, the Caledonian "Dunalastair" reached Princes Street after a 121 minute run. This gave an arrival some eight minutes early.

The second racer which might have been seen in the Citadel simultaneously with the West Coast train, would have been the 09.30 from St Pancras – arriving five minutes early. According to the *Carlisle Journal*, the Midland express "was telegraphed six minutes early passing Appleby", although one minute appears to have been lost in the thirty miles from there to Carlisle. It entered the Citadel station "horsed by one of the new engines of large type", as the *Journal* delightfully put it, adding that the 132 minutes for the run from Leeds and 370 minutes for the 308½ miles from London constituted a record for the Midland.

Talavera may just have drawn up at the facing platform as the North British got under way, strictly on schedule. An uneventful 135 minute run appears to have resulted on the Waverley Route, but this of course was certain to lead to a conflict with the *Flying Scotsman* at Portobello East if the North Eastern kept up their efforts to reach Edinburgh as near 18.00 as possible.

This was how one newspaper correspondent in Edinburgh saw the contest developing:

> "Both the Midland and the East Coast trains, which arrive at Waverley, were signalled as having crossed the Border at time, and speculation was rife amongst those on the (Waverley) platform as to which would have the advantage of the clear signal outside of Portobello. It was thought that the Midland express would get any (advantage) that was going..."

It would come as no great surprise to him, then, to see the North British train "winding itself out of the Calton tunnel", and draw to a punctual standstill for the first time since the service was inaugurated. The reporter recorded that the North Eastern arrived exactly four minutes later but he went on to make the following comment about the North Eastern express which is of considerable interest to the railway historian:

> "In the last stages of the journey the train was brought to a stand near Portobello, owing to signals being against it. A delay of four minutes was occasioned, and the express arrived in the Waverley exactly four minutes after the Midland".

Sixty years after the 1901 Race former LMS Pacific No. 46254 City of Stoke-on-Trent *stands at the north end of Carlisle Citadel station in the summer of 1961. Here on the final day of the 1901 Race, the Midland/NBR and West Coast trains stood almost side by side. "Jinty" 0-6-0 tank No. 47505 shares the scene with this magnificent Pacific. (Author)*

This inevitably gives rise to speculation as to whether the North British held up the rival express to ensure the punctual arrival of their own train. Portobello East junction is three and a half miles from Waverley, and greatly reduced in importance nowadays since the closure of the Waverley Route in 1969. (See Appendix C.) The distance from here to Waverley could be covered by either train in 1901 in about 4½ minutes pass to stop or in six minutes start to stop. Anything less – such as NER 4-4-0 No 1621's hair-raising 60mph dash in 1895 – risked an uncomfortable negotiation of trackwork west of Portobello station and there was also the 1¼ miles of 1 in 78 to be climbed from St Margaret's into Waverley.

It seems likely that, given a clear road, the North British train would have passed through the junction between 18.00 and 18.01, to achieve a punctual arrival at Waverley four minutes later. However, if its North Eastern rival had been held at the East junction for four minutes and still entered Waverley only four minutes after the 09.30, it must have reached the junction at 17.59! (Four minutes standing, then six minutes start to stop). Not only that, but a possible passing time at the junction, had there been no braking, would probably have been up to ninety seconds earlier.

What happened in that tall 45-lever box high above the tracks at Portobello on that summer evening? O.S. Nock assured his readers of *The Railway Race to the North* that the Portobello signalman was not called upon to choose between two fast-approaching racers, in the manner of the Caledonian signalman at Kinnaber six years earlier. On that occasion, so the story goes, both trains approached simultaneously, but the Caledonian employee sportingly gave the road to the rival North British express. As Mr Nock indicated, there was no possibility of any such thing happening on the eastern outskirts of Edinburgh.

If the NBR's attitude appears to have been unsporting, it should be recalled that their rival was honouring neither its published timetable nor the 8¼ hr schedule limit agreed between the East and West Coast companies in 1896. So one can be forgiven for appearing cynical in concluding that the North British would unhesitatingly delay the *Flying Scotsman* to favour the train worked by its own engine and men, if only to emphasise to the North Eastern the need to seek agreement on timetabling over the Berwick-Edinburgh section.

In any event, the proximity of those signalboxes south of Portobello East would probably have favoured the Waverley Route train anyway in the event of an actual or near-simultaneous arrival of the two trains. The boxes communicating with Portobello East on both routes southwards were Niddrie North (then named Brunstane Park) on the Waverley Route, and Joppa on the East Coast main-line. The former was approximately three-quarters of a mile distant, Joppa merely a third of that distance, and within sight of the junction. It seems likely that the North Eastern train would have had to travel closer to the vital junction, before its presence was advised to the East box, than its victorious rival. Such hypothesis does not allow for the North British management's policy of teaching the North Eastern a lesson by delaying their trains; something obvious even to the expectant spectators on the Waverley platforms.

July 8th was the climax of the 1901 contest with the topic vanishing completely from the newspapers. The *Railway Magazine* summed it up with a cartoon captioned "Well, we've had a friendly splutter and that's all". Perhaps with the North British "winning" at last, pride was considered satisfied on all sides.

Portobello East junction in 1981. This early morning shot in October of that year shows Class 40 No. 40 015, formerly named Lusitania, *bringing the 08.10 from Newcastle towards Edinburgh. The greatly diminished status of the junction is apparent, with the Waverley Route/Suburban Circle turn-off reduced to a single line. (M. Macdonald)*

Portobello nowadays has a much reduced railway presence, compared to this 1961 view. The main-lines to Edinburgh (in the background) were quadrupled here, following the joining of the East Coast and Waverley routes at the East junction, becoming double again just west of Portobello station in the right background. The yards are now a memory, echoed by the recent closure of the Freighliner depot, and seen here are 2MT 2-6-0 No. 46462 on a trip working and a N15 tank shunting the p.w. yard. (Author)

AFTERMATH

Railway historians have always been wary of describing the 1901 competition between London and Edinburgh as a "race", and many of them have ignored the episode altogether. This prompts a number of questions. Was there really a race? If so, was it no more than a clash of timetables? Why did it stop? What resulted from it?

Firstly, was there really a race? Charles Rous-Martin said there most certainly was not, but then he was writing for an issue of *The Engineer* published on July 5th, before he knew of the West Coast entry into the fray. It is a tribute to the respect, if not awe, in which "CRM" has always been held by subsequent writers on railway matters that his negative analysis has become the received opinion about the 1901 competition.

O.S. Nock, in his *Railway Race to the North*, and Cecil J. Allen in *The North Eastern Railway* both dismiss 1901 as unworthy of their detailed attention. In particular, the latter author has been fairly scathing about the NBR's performance in July 1901, something which hardly seems justified by a retrospective assessment based on existing knowledge, or on the Carlisle newspaper's view of Waverley Route running at the time.

It seems inconceivable that the LNWR and Caledonian should run so hard on the 5th, if there was no will to reach the Scottish capital first – and such will to be first means a "race" in anyone's language! Also to be considered are the NBR's published figures about the time-keeping of the 09.30 down, and some of this data is listed in the Appendix A. Its main implication is that up to and including July 8th, the North British was

39

prepared to run very hard to regain time lost south of Carlisle or in the Citadel station itself, where the change-over from vacuum to Westinghouse brake could barely be accomplished in the scheduled five minutes.

In the first seven days of the accelerated 09.30's life, the NBR saved twenty-four minutes on the Waverley Route, despite the severity of the schedule. In contrast, the next seven runs saw a *total* of only one minute recovered. The table is included to illustrate this particular point; otherwise the company's figures do not always tally with those published in the various newspapers, and are quite uncomplimentary to the issuing company, particularly for the runs on the 1st and 8th.

Was 1901, then, just a clash of timetables? Probably, but it happened at a time of some tension between the NB and NER. In contrast, nine years later, the relative arrival times at Portobello East were actually tighter, with only a five minute interval between the St Pancras and the *Flying Scotsman*. But by 1910 the Berwick-Edinburgh running powers dispute was no longer a source of contention, having been settled in the English company's favour by the agreement of 1904.

This makes the West Coast's entry in the race all the more puzzling. If the race was caused solely by the practical need to reach Portobello East first and establish a "pathing" priority from there into Waverley, obviously the LNWR and Caledonian need not feel threatened. One contemporary writer, R.E. Charlewood, recorded in 1902 that early arrivals at Carlisle could easily be achieved by northbound LNWR expresses in the previous year "had not strict orders been issued ... to prohibit anything that could possibly be termed 'racing'".

But it appears that the press, particularly the *Daily Mail*, may have been responsible for the West's entry – since the Princes Street arrival times were being reported along with the racing rivals at Waverley, the LNWR and Caledonian performances appeared in a poor light. More pertinently however, the North Eastern's determination to accelerate their express through the 8¼ hour "barrier" was a considerable threat.

It should be emphasised that York's determination to reach Edinburgh by an unofficial scheduled time of six o'clock was not universal knowledge. As far as the travelling public was concerned, the NER appeared to trying to reach Edinburgh as far ahead of time as possible – so they must be racing someone!

Why did the race stop when it did? The North British was in a hopelessly anomalous position regarding this rivalry, and must surely have welcomed its end. It was of course a partner in the East Coast consortium in the operation of such expresses as the *Flying Scotsman*, contributing to the construction and upkeep of its rolling-stock. Given the release by the NBR of the unflattering punctuality record of the 09.30, it may well be that the Edinburgh company was simply indulging in a bit of muscle-flexing that July. On the one hand it was reminding King's Cross and York that it had an alternative route to London, while on the other, emphasising to

Derby that herculean efforts north of Carlisle were perhaps not worth the effort for the North British in an alliance of dubious economic value. It may well be that the NBR was not too anxious to make the new service appear a success, for "diplomatic" reasons – to emphasise the NBR's operating difficulties undertaken on behalf of a demanding ally. On the other hand perhaps such an attitude was less than fair to the Midland. When the latter company was having second thoughts in the late 1860s about the value of its proposed Settle-Carlisle line, its Scottish allies were quick to dispel such faint-heartedness and kept Derby to its promise of a new Anglo-Scottish route.

As the unofficial passenger figures published in *The Scotsman* for July 1901 show, there was a question-mark against the viability of the Midland/North British long-distance passenger services. While revenue certainly improved each August — we know of at least one occasion when the overnight St Pancras-Edinburgh express had to be run in no fewer than six portions – daytime loadings may have been unacceptably light for eleven months of the year. Between 1903 and 1907 the Midland paid the North British some £11,000 in subsidy for maintaining their share of operating the 13.30 and 19.20 down expresses. (Incidentally, the Midland's share in the Forth Bridge Company, which was responsible for building that great structure and in maintaining it up to Nationalisation in 1948, was actually greater than that of the Great Northern and North Eastern companies! Yet the East Coast companies were the beneficiaries in terms of shorter distances and reduced journey times to Dundee and Aberdeen, while the Midland was paying a subsidy to the NBR for some of its own Anglo-Scottish services. Was the Midland's involvement in such traffic worth the expense?)

Given the often unremunerative nature of Waverley Route trains, there would be little point in the Edinburgh company working men and machines to their limits just to save a few minutes. It did not help matters commercially that there was so little apparent initiative by the M & NB in their timetabling of Anglo-Scottish expresses, which tended to echo the departure times of the Coast route trains. Surely an early morning departure from Edinburgh southwards – up to two hours earlier than the 09.25 – would have been more profitable, in a society where most people where up and about by 7 a.m. anyway, particularly in the summer months in those halcyon years before the introduction of British Summer Time in 1916? Additionally, a London arrival well before the existing time of quarter past six would be useful to the southbound traveller. And even a 2.30 p.m. departure from St Pancras could still have given a reasonable arrival time in both the major Scottish cities before midnight.

One interesting contemporary theory about the sudden end to the race was W.J. Scott's belief that the West Coast were simply not good enough to compete! After the impressive arrival at Princes Street station in 7 hours 40 minutes on the 5th, the North Eastern brought their next available northbound train – the overnight 20.15 ex-King's Cross – into Waverley in four minutes less. Yet the Reverend Scott, whom O.S. Nock sagely divined as an East Coast admirer, believed that there was no need to respond to the West Coast's run, on the (to him) justifiable grounds that it had not been very impressive. This is a strange verdict on the fastest daytime run of the year, particularly in view of the possible nett arrival time of around five thirty.

Perhaps he was more accurate six years previously when, writing about restaurant car-equipped trains, he predicted

> "it is hardly likely that a true 'race' will ever happen with these excellent trains; a swerve or sudden check at seventy-five an hour would not help to make 'good digestion wait on appetite', even in a 12-wheel dining-saloon".

The introduction of dining-cars had enforced major timetabling changes in the last decade of the nineteenth century, doing away with the need for meal-stops of twenty or thirty minutes duration. The Midland, for example, had been in the habit of feeding its Anglo-Scottish passengers at Normanton, with both up and down passengers having their hunger satisfied simultaneously. Dining-cars did away with such stops, although there was no immediate resulting acceleration in the case of the East Coast trains. But when it is remembered that the problem of dining steadily at speed was never satisfactorily solved in the steam age – perhaps not even now – reluctance to commit restaurant-car expresses to intensified racing in 1901 is understandable.

Although this brief outburst of Anglo-Scottish railway racing does not deserve the oblivion into which it has apparently been consigned, purists of railway history will be quick to point out that the 1901 episode involved average speeds little better than those achieved by less powerful locomotives in previous years; indeed the 1888 running times were inflated by the need to stop to water the engines and feed the passengers. But this is to overlook the fact that 1888 was a comparatively well-planned campaign of gradual, and then more pronounced, accelerations – a mobilisation of resources which involved directors, managers, inspectors and footplate crews. In contrast, 1901 was more a result of clashing timetables producing individual initiatives by the man on the spot, whether footplate crew or signal staff.

If the 1888 and 1895 races enabled the locomotive designers and the company timetablers to glimpse the potential for fast inter-city travel, what was learned from the 1901 contest? It is quite possible that one of the most fundamental aspects of modern rail operation – train control – was the product of the 1901 episode.

Although pioneered in the USA, train control – the remote management of railway operations from a centre equipped with telecommunications – was introduced into this country by the Midland Railway. It was plainly illogical for such a major company to even attempt to integrate a myriad of untimetabled coal trains into the blood-stream of a system carrying long-distance passenger traffic at maximum speed. It seems incredible, but was certainly true in 1901, that Midland coal trains, with no scheduled times to observe, started or continued their journeys whenever local inspectors thought it convenient. The company's management at Derby eventually woke up to the possibilities of Control and established the country's first centre, on an initially experimental basis, at Masborough (Rotherham) in 1907.

Not too surprisingly, its ally the North British became the first Scottish company to follow suit. After setting up a control system for their Lothians coal traffic, one of the NB superintendents was able to report to his General Manager in 1913 "the system is fast realising in a large degree all the benefits that were expected from it", and that was even before telephone facilities had been fitted.

This first Scottish Control centre was situated at Portobello, less than a mile from the "winning post" for the 1901 Railway Race to Edinburgh.

An unidentified Holmes 4-4-0 of the North British Railway speeds southwards through Fountainhall with an Edinburgh-Carlisle express on the Waverley Route around 1910. On the right a Drummond R Class 4-4-0 tank waits to leave on a Lauder branch train, Nowadays both the main-line and branch are nothing more than weedbound trackbeds. (Clapperton Photos, Selkirk).

APPENDIX A: THE TABLES

THE "PLACINGS" 1901

	First	Second	Third	Margin (Mins)
July 1st	NE	NB	–	4
2nd	NE	NB	–	15
3rd	NE	NB	–	6
4th	NE	NB	–	12
5th	CR	NE	NB	29
6th	CR	NE	NB	8
8th	NB	CR	NE	2

ARRIVAL TIMES OF LONDON-EDINBURGH EXPRESSES AT EDINBURGH TERMINI FROM JULY 1ST-6TH, AND ON JULY 8TH, 1901.

Arrival at:	Waverley		Princes St.
	GN/NE	M/NB	LNW/C
Scheduled at:	18.15	18.05	18.15
Mon. 1st.	18.02	18.06	18.34
Tues. 2nd.	18.03	18.18	18.30
Wed. 3rd.	18.09	18.15	18.17
Thurs. 4th.	18.07	18.19	18.15
Fri. 5th.	18.09	18.12	17.40
Sat. 6th.	18.06	18.15	17.58
Mon. 8th.	18.09	18.05	18.07

Sources: *Railway Times/Scotsman.*

NORTH BRITISH RAILWAY STATISTICS FOR ARRIVALS OF 09.30 ex-ST PANCRAS AT EDINBURGH WAVERLEY, July 1901, SHOWING TIME GAINED NORTH OF CARLISLE.

		Carlisle arr.	Carlisle dep.	Edin. arr.	Mins +
July	1st	9 late	10 late	1 late	9
	2nd	15	21	13	8
	3rd	12	13	10	3
	4th	13	16	14	2
	5th	6	8	7	1
	6th	8	11	10	1
	8th	(5)	0	1	0
	9th	0	0	(1)	1
	10th	8	10	10	0
	11th	3	7	7	0
	12th	2	4	4	0
	13th	7	10	10	0
	15th	3	6	7	0
	16th	0	3	1	2
	17th	5	7	7	0
	18th	(2)	0	0	0
	19th	5	10	8	2
	20th	5	7	6	1

Figures in brackets indicate early arrivals.

These records of the 09.30's running do not strictly accord with those made by other observers, and are in fact not biased in the NBR's favour. They are included here to indicate the falling-away of the NBR effort after July 8th, the last column only itemising minutes gained running from Carlisle to ensure a punctual arrival.

APPENDIX B : LOGS

PROGRESS OF 09.30 ST. PANCRAS – EDINBURGH
JULY 1st 1901

MIDLAND RAILWAY : LEEDS-CARLISLE

Load: 7 coaches, approx 190 tons gross.
Engine: 2606 class 4-4-0, identity unknown.

	Miles	Minutes	Av. Speed
Leeds			
Skipton	26	29	53¾
Settle	41½	48½	47½
Ribblehead	52	68¼	35
Blea Moor	53¼	70¾	30
Dent	58	78½	36¾
Hawes Jct	61¼	82	55¾
Appleby	82½	101	67
Lazonby	97¼	114	68
Carlisle	112¾	131	54¾

NORTH BRITISH RAILWAY
CARLISLE – EDINBURGH   (WAVERLEY)

Load: 5 bogies, 150 tons gross.   Schedule: 135 mins., non-stop.
Loco: Class M 4-4-0 No 738.

	mls.	mins.	mph
Carlisle			
Longtown	9½	12¼	46(av.)
Riddings Jct.	14¼	17½	62
Riccarton Jct.	32½	45	39(av.)
Hawick	45½	62	45(av.)
St Boswells	57¾	76¼	64
Melrose	61	—	6l
Galashiels	64¾	83½	slow
Heriot	79	103	44(av.)
Portobello (station)	95¼	122	5l(av.)
Edinburgh Waverley	98¼	126	45(av.)

APPENDIX C : PORTOBELLO EAST JUNCTION

Portobello East is not perhaps the most famous rail junction in Scotland, although it probably deserves to be. For it was here in 1847 that the modern remote-control concept of rail signalling was pioneered; something which seems so obvious nowadays as to cause wonder than any alternative was ever contemplated.

It seems that in 1847 Robert Skelden, charged with the task of looking after a pair of signals at the NBR's new Hawick Junction at Portobello, rigged up a counter-balancing apparatus, comprising discarded track chairs, which would allow him to operate the signals from a central vantage point.

Legend has it that this laziness – for so the management regarded it – nearly lost the inventive signalman his job. After all, he was supposed to stay beside his signal and operate it manually. But the potential of Skelden's idea was soon grasped by his superiors, and signalling took a quantum leap in the direction of its present status of electronic remote train control. The Royal Scottish Society of Arts rewarded Skelden's innovation with a silver medal "worth five sovereigns" on November 2nd 1849, "for his description, drawing, and working model, of a 'railway-signal and method of working it at a considerable distance from the station'." But there is no record of his having protected it by patent, something which could conceivably have made him a very rich man.

Until 1852 the British patent system was chaotic, and particularly discriminated against Scottish and Irish inventors. An attempt to patent a device or process in Scotland was both expensive and ineffective in preventing unlicensed use elsewhere in the United Kingdom. Complete British protection was almost prohibitively expensive for all but the richest citizens, before reforms in the patent system were carried out, not surprisingly inspired by such inventive Scots as Sir David Brewster and Lord Brougham.

Portobello East junction is much reduced in size and importance nowadays. A single facing crossover suffices to connect the down line with the Freightliner turnoff, which also acts as the junction for traffic from South Leith bypassing the depot. Freightliners ceased to call here from 1987, making 46 men redundant, and this signalled the end of freight operations in the Portobello area after 140 years. Yet as late as 1979 the depot had been handling 2,700 containers monthly, and was profitable at the time of closure on Saturday April 4th 1987. The main-line has been relaid to ease the considerable curves caused by the former existence of Portobello station a little farther on. The main-line itself is only double, in comparison to the four-track section which used to be necessary to carry the line's capacity before the rationalisation of the 1970s.

SOURCES CONSULTED

Allen, C.J. *The North Eastern Railway*. Ian Allan, 1964.
Barnes, E.G. *The Midland Main Line, 1875-1922*. Allen & Unwin.
Bell, R. *Twenty-five years of the North Eastern Railway*. Railway
   Gazette, 1951.
Cornwell, H.J.C. *Forty years of Caledonian locomotives, 1882-1922*.
Ellis, C.H. *The North British Railway*. 2nd edn. Ian Allan, 1959.
Hoole, K. *North Eastern Locomotive Sheds*. David & Charles.
Nock, O.S. *The Caledonian Dunalastairs and associated classes*. David &
   Charles, 1968.
———————— *The Premier Line: the story of London and North Western
   locomotives*. Ian Allan, 1952.
————————*The Railway Race to the North*. 2nd edn. Ian Allan, 1976.
Railway Correspondence and Travel Society. *Locomotives of the
   London and North Eastern Railway*. Vols. 2b, 3b, and 4.
Thomas, J. *The North British Railway*. Vol. II. David & Charles, 1975.

Newspapers and Magazines; *Carlisle Journal, Carlisle Patriot, The
   Engineer, Glasgow Herald, Herapath's Railway Journal, Newcastle
   Evening Chronicle, Pall Mall Gazette, Railway Magazine, Railway
   Times, The Scotsman*.

Ordnance Survey Maps for Edinburgh, 1896 and 1906.

Scottish Record Office files; BR/NBR/1/135, 1/367, 1/385, 4/224, 8/1078,
   8/1399. RHP26662.

The author wishes to acknowledge the assistance given him in preparing this book by Mr. G. Barbour and his colleagues at the Scottish Record Office, by the staffs of Carlisle and Edinburgh city libraries, the National Library of Scotland, and by Mr. R. B. Lacey. Scotsman Publications Ltd have kindly given permission to quote from relevant issues of *The Scotsman*.